A Ringing of Bells

A Conversational Fantasy

Christopher Fry

SAMUELFRENCH-LONDON.CO.UK
SAMUELFRENCH.COM

ISBN 978-0-573-12207-1

www.samuelfrench-london.co.uk

www.samuelfrench.com

FOR AMATEUR PRODUCTION ENQUIRIES

UNITED KINGDOM AND WORLD
EXCLUDING NORTH AMERICA
plays@SamuelFrench-London.co.uk
020 7255 4302/01

Each title is subject to availability from Samuel French,

depending upon country of performance.

CHARACTERS

Eve
Adam
Receptionist
George
Paul
Elizabeth

The action of the play takes place in a small village hotel

Time: Millennium Eve

Written for and dedicated to the boys of my
old school, Bedford Modern School

Christopher Fry

A RINGING OF BELLS

The entrance hall of a hotel, Elstow. It is midnight

The church bells are ringing, with great certainty as the play begins, but then intermittently as the wind takes them

The Receptionist is at the desk, scarcely noticeable: he has fallen asleep

Through the door come a man and a woman: we will call them Adam and Eve

Eve But where is it? Where have we come to? Why don't you tell me? You must know.

Adam Well, that's the trouble. I don't.

Eve You must have known which way you were driving.

Adam Eve, you'd better sit down, I think.

Eve Why, what is it?

Adam That's the question. When we set out, this was going to be a perfectly pleasant and sensible evening. We were going to celebrate——

Eve New Year's Eve. Well, exactly. But somewhere where we knew where we were, I should have thought.

Adam Well, they're ringing the bells, whoever they are. There's nothing strange about that. It's what my watch says—just gone midnight. So there's nothing wrong with the time.

Eve What do you mean, wrong with the time? Why should there be? For goodness sake, what are you trying to tell me?

Adam (*taking the help of a chair*) Just now—driving over—you didn't feel nervous?

Eve No, why should I feel nervous? I've never felt nervous when you were driving. Only I wanted to know where we were going. That's why I kept asking you. Where were we making for? And you wouldn't say anything except "Well". You kept saying "Well". You wouldn't tell me.

Adam How could I, when I didn't know?

Eve (*sitting beside him*) You must have known which road we were on. You must have known where you were making for.

Adam I've got to tell you. I wasn't driving.

Eve Adam, stop teasing me. You know you were driving.

Adam I know I had my hands on the steering wheel, I know that. And I didn't feel we were out of control: not totally, anyway. But there was a kind of *persuasion*—a kind of calling almost—running through my hands.

Eve Well, why didn't you say so? I should have told you to pull into a lay-by until you felt all right again.

Adam But I didn't feel wrong, Eve. I felt in good hands—except that the hands were my own hands. You don't think I'm crazy?

Eve Well, I do in a way, yes, I do. Or else the car is. I'll try to make some sense of it, given help. Only, I'd like to know where we have come to. And why the steering wheel was so keen on getting here. (*She gets up as though to look for someone*) There must be somebody to ask, though this hotel, if it is a hotel, seems strangely deserted for a New Year's Eve—particularly this New Year. Oh, there *is* somebody, dead asleep by the look of him: that's not very receiving for a receptionist. Shall we wake him?

Adam Better *you* don't—he might wonder what he was waking up to. (*He goes across and rings the desk bell*) Hallo there.

The Receptionist jerks into life

I'm sorry to interrupt anything.

Receptionist No, no, you mustn't mind that. It's been a particularly busy evening.

Adam (*looking round the deserted room*) Really?

Receptionist For thoughts. They come swarming in, and don't really leave each other enough room to reach a conclusion.

Adam Perhaps I can help. My friend and I—we were wondering where we are.

Receptionist Yes, of course—it's only natural.

Adam Well, will you tell us, please, so that we can get our bearings?

Receptionist I expect you mean *exactly* where.

Adam Yes, of course exactly where.

Receptionist You mean this building?

Adam All right—this building to start with.

Receptionist And that depends, as you know, on whereabouts in time you are standing.

Eve Adam, let's leave here—why can't he be civil?

Adam Look, we've already been a bit thrown out of kilter this evening—just be good enough to tell us——

Receptionist I was meaning to be helpful. Time covers a great distance, you know. If you are meaning to concentrate on the particular hour which has just landed us on to the third millennium——

Adam For heaven's sake, yes, of course we do.

Receptionist Then we can't call this place *The Star and Saracen*, which at another time we might have done. Or *The Catherine Wheel*, which was possible once. It could more reasonably be called *The Chequers* where you think you are now—"the chequer board of nights and days", as the poet said—though *The Red Lion* across the Green could be equally suitable. John Newold did well for himself there, and the Newold family held it across a century or more—which is why I said New-old makes that pub a suitable resting place in the ocean of time if that doesn't sound fanciful——

Eve gives a little scream of exasperation

Am I confusing your friend?

Adam Suppose you make things simpler for her by just telling us the name of the village.

Receptionist Oh, yes, there's no difficulty there, whichever vantage point you're taking—not at least unless we go back fifteen hundred years or so——

Adam For God's sake, man, what *is* it?

Receptionist Well, in the Old English it meant the place of assembly, the holy place—belonging, it's thought, to someone possibly called——

Adam The name, man, the name of the village!

Receptionist Which I was just telling you. It's Elstow.

Adam Good grief. Is it really? (*To Eve*) I was brought here when I was a kid. On some special occasion, I think, though I don't remember… How did my hands know that?

Eve Adam, be sensible. Things don't happen like that.

Adam But someone brought me here before. And something brought me here tonight. Someone brought me and helped me to paint a picture of the church. Or rather, of the bell tower. (*To the Receptionist*) That's it, isn't it? The bell tower stands on its own—like an individual standing for what he believes. I mean, as though the bells spoke for themselves.

Eve Well, to speak for myself I can see what might have happened—your subconscious knew the road and so you just followed it.

Adam But I was a small boy then, and someone brought me—I don't know how we got here.

Eve There must be some perfectly sensible answer. There are always sensible answers if you keep your head and look for them.

Adam What do we know about quantum mechanics?

Eve Absolutely nothing, and rather glad of it.

Adam Suppose the voice of the bells—I mean the vibrations—through the darkness without the daylight to interrupt them—broke through some kind of floodgate which kept time from interflowing—the way this chap seemed to be describing.

Eve If you're thinking of becoming a little boy painting pictures, where does that leave *me*? Come on, Adam, let's try to be sensible.

Adam After two thousand years, time must be wearing a bit thin.

Eve Well, don't lean on it, for heaven's sake.

Adam I wonder how old those bells are, how much of history they have been talking to.

A man, George, comes in through the door

Receptionist Here's somebody who should be able to tell you. Were you one of the bell-ringers tonight, George?

George Yes, I was, along with Paul Cobb, but I'll tell you something: as well as us two——

Receptionist This gentleman was asking how long the bells have hung there.

George I could tell you—given time to remember—the sixteen hundreds all bar one—but I'll tell you this: while we was ringing—we'd been ringing five minutes or so, I should say—there was another chap had joined us—I hadn't noticed him coming up into the loft—nobody I could name, though there was something familiar about him. He just stood there listening—and now and then his arms would lift as though he was one with us. Hey, I thought, you know something about it, and I looked across at Paul and jerked my head towards this fellow, but old Paul didn't seem to notice him, and when we was done and I turned to speak to him he was gone, the fellow. He's not been in here, then—a foreigner, you've not seen him around?

Receptionist A foreigner, no, I've seen no foreigner.

George I don't mean a foreign foreigner, I mean foreign to these parts, like. And yet again he wasn't so foreign—like I said, there was something familiar. Maybe it was something about what he was wearing that seemed out of the way, though I couldn't get more than a look while I was ringing. A sizeable fellow, he seemed to be. You haven't seen him, then?

Receptionist No, I haven't seen any sizeable fellow.

George You wouldn't think one of his build would just vanish.

Receptionist Well, whatever our build, it's a way we have in the end. But no, you wouldn't think so. Not if he was actually here.

Eve (*to George*) Had the night cleared up at all when you came in? It was so misty, a small rain almost, when we were driving here.

George Yes, trying to make the beacon catch was quite a business, for the damp wood. But then it leapt up fine, and the heat of it seemed to break up the mist as well, and we've got the night sky back with us.

Eve (*to Adam*) Because I would like to see where you have brought me to. And you would too, to find out how much you remember.

Adam (*to George*) I was just telling her—I was brought here as a child—on a day trip I suppose it must have been. That's going back a bit. But it's all begun to ring a bell with me. It was the oldest of my aunts who brought me—goodness, yes— (*to the Receptionist*) and talk about time covering a distance: she told me once that she had sat on the lap of a great-uncle who had been patted on the head by George the Fourth—so that when I held her hand we were making a bridge——

Receptionist You could almost walk across.

Eve Well, let's walk through the village, Adam—that's going to be easier.

Adam Yes, in a minute. Things are beginning to come together. I remember now why she brought me here. She had been reading *The Pilgrim's Progress* to me, and getting me to read some of it to her—nice big type, I remember—had been in the family for a century at least—well, I remember an inscription on the fly-leaf—beautiful writing—Christmas 1863—and yet as immaculate as on the day it was published. I had to go and wash my hands before I turned the pages.

George So you know, don't you, that this village——

Adam Yes, that's what I mean—it's John Bunyan's village—which is why she brought me here. He was born here, wasn't he?

George Well, within a mile or two, yes. Lived and married here, and put us all into history.

Paul Cobb enters from within the hotel

But here's the man to tell you about him—I'd lost track of you, Paul, after the ringing. I've just told this gentleman, you're the history bloke.

Paul Good evening. What's the question?

Adam No, I've just realized how I knew about this village—because of Bunyan.

Paul Ah, yes, the sturdy John. I've pretty well lived his life with him over the years. And tonight especially I thought of him. At one time of his life, as a lad, he would have had his head off his shoulders with joy at bell-ringing. The time when he would dance like a demon, swear like a tinker, play games on a Sunday like a champion. But when he saw these things as sins which were driving him into an eternity of Hell, why then, poor fellow, he thought the bells would fall on him and strike him dead.

Adam But tonight you think it would have made him glad to hear them ringing out so clear through the darkness?

Paul Yes. When he had lost his terrors he would have been eager to be up with us there, telling the night that the two thousand years of Christ had come. I could just see him there.

George What do you mean, Paul, you could just see him?

Paul I can guess how he would have gone for it, singing out the old, and ringing in the new. And, as well as that, celebrating the three hundred and twenty-two anniversaries of his book. That would have put him in a glow, I don't doubt it.

George That's all you meant, was it?

Adam I used to have a recurring dream—a nightmare—when I was very small. I would dream I was trying to escape from a town that was going to explode—or a city about to be bombed, perhaps it was. And it was desperately difficult to hurry because the path I was on was the keyboard of a piano. And what made it even more scary, more difficult, was that I'd been told to keep to the black notes. It used to wake me up in a panic. I hadn't thought of it till now.

Paul How about that? Escaping from the City of Destruction.

Eve Poor little Adam.

Adam Or I think more likely what I'd heard from my parents about the last War and the bombing of cities. Or, strangely enough, even more fearfully about the first Great War, from my grandfather. It's as if I had been a part of that time, as vivid as that. As though time was a tide coming back to where I played on the beach. Do you hear that, Mr Receptionist? Blow me down, if he hasn't gone to sleep again.

Eve You wouldn't think there was enough dream-space to accommodate him!

Paul Perhaps we are the dream that he's having.

George I keep thinking of that fellow who was watching us while we was bell-ringing. But you didn't see him, Paul, or did you?

Adam My God, things don't change much, do they, with the passing of time? In those kid nightmares I had all those years ago I was like a refugee from Bosnia or somewhere. That crazy division of human beings because of their labels! Do you think humans were more as they were meant to be in 1914? I'm thinking of that first Christmas, before the armies were thigh-deep in slaughter—when the Germans started singing: *Stille Nacht, Heilige Nacht*—and the British took it up—*Silent Night, Holy Night*—and they played football together. But then there were those four murderous years to follow. At least that wasn't the kind of destruction that John Bunyan was fearful of.

Paul Well, no. The Civil War caught him for a couple of years, of course. He was conscripted when he was sixteen, called up by one side or the other. I don't think he ever said which.

George It would have been Cromwell's lot, surely?

Paul Maybe—or he might have got hauled in when the King was making a progress through the county. But no—it was later—it was the civil war in himself that so tore him apart.

Adam Yes, not being on good terms with himself, that was hard. (*To Eve*) So: shall we go out into the night and see what we can find there?

Eve No, I don't think we need to go just yet.

Adam Only I thought you were anxious to move on.

Eve (*laughing*) Well, I don't have to be everything you think. There are things I'm interested to hear. (*To Paul*) Was there a wife? No, I see: he was only eighteen when he came out of the army. But then——

Paul He married at twenty, I think it was. And just travelled around, as his father had done, mending pots, the tinker's trade. But from what we know he had a great relish for life. He played a fiddle and a flute—maybe that helped the poet that was in him to take over when the time came—that and reading the chap-books that his grandfather peddled round the villages, and the Bible that brought him to think he was on the way to damnation. There was that shattering moment out here on the Green when he was playing tipcat on a Sunday. He was just taking a strike at the cat when, as he said, "a voice did suddenly dart from Heaven into my soul, and it was as if I'd seen the Lord Jesus looking down, severely threatening me with punishment for all my ungodly practices". That's the load he gave to Christian when he came to write his book.

Adam And that's when the joy even went out of the bell-ringing.

Eve He couldn't have been exactly a little ray of sunshine to his wife.

Paul Well, he was as alive as a man could be, whether when he was wrong and guilt-ridden, or when, as he did later on, he came to see that humour was a great lifter of loads: when his God became not a breaker-in but a bringer-out.

Eve God does seem to me to be a ridiculously small word for the size of creation. I imagine it was a pretty comfortably-sized universe in Bunyan's time. A kind of upstairs-downstairs job. But when you think of what infinities we're beginning to reach out to now, always further, always the immeasurable power and the glory.

Adam The Big Bang, and all that came of it.

George Or from what I hear they're saying now—Stephen Hawking or who is it—an almighty tiny bang—all space and time and evolution out of the compression of a germ you can't begin to imagine.

Adam Like one little sound suddenly becoming all the languages. In the beginning was the word, and the word was with God, and the word was God.

Paul And what I do know is, there couldn't be an energy strong enough to create, unless it was set off by purpose—the great, grinding, accomplishing of purpose—making, destroying, remaking, adjusting, persuading...

Eve The beauty and the horror of it. Sun rising, moon setting, moon rising, sun setting, like the scales of justice.

Adam And the extravaganza of the inventiveness of life. Into every nook and cranny. I saw an insect yesterday, walking across the white piece of paper I was about to write on, honestly no bigger than a dot I could make with my pen, but with tentacles and feet, making its way within the millions of light-years. And the heavenly eccentricity of a peacock's tail. How on earth did a common sex-urge turn itself into such a pattern of eyes in a shimmer of feathers? Nobody's ever found a word, have they, for what produces such a conjuring of music out of a bird's egg? Well, yes, I know: the survival of the fittest, and all that. But what *does* it—the brain? The sex genes? The mind? What is "the mind", anyway?

Paul I've asked myself the same question. "Consciousness", the dictionary says; and "intelligence". No great help. A kind of creative discipleship, perhaps.

Eve But the horror—I'm sorry to come back to that. The remorseless savagery that seems so to contradict the wonder. I could do without that.

Paul Well, what's in a victory that's unopposed? Tempering the metal with heat and cool and heat. The positive and negative that makes things work. All that. As it took Bunyan's despair and terror to forge the power of his writing.

Eve All I can say is, I think creation seriously overdid it.

Paul (*laughing*) Pretty seriously. Strange as it is, I suppose the darker the shadow, the brighter the light that casts it.

George Well, he had the horrors all right, did old Bunyan, when he thought that the bell he was ringing would come down and crush him.

Paul He certainly went through it. And as soon as he came through on the sunny side, delighting the Meeting House with his preaching, the Bedford Meeting was closed down, and the local Justice issued a warrant for his arrest. Suddenly, instead of being, as he had been, the sinner in his own conscience, now—at peace with his God—he was thrown into jail a sinner in his country's politics. Even with the fear of transportation in his mind, and his family getting destitute.

Adam But they must at least have given him pen and paper.

Paul Later they did.

Adam And he wrote his book. He wouldn't have had the chance of it this century—if he had been prisoner of war on the Burma Railway, or brought down to skin and bone in a concentration camp.

Eve Transportation? Would they really have done that to him, for not keeping to the rules?

Paul And worse. The statute said that if, after being transported, he returned to England, he would suffer death as a felon. In his imagination, he said, he was often on the ladder with the rope about his neck.

George An odd thing about a lot of human beings. They can't bear it if anybody's different from themselves. Like they want to live in a world entirely populated by mirrors.

Adam Delight in difference—who said that? But as if disease, earthquakes, drought, flood weren't enough to contend with, you have to add civil war and ethnic cleansing to make life even more unbearable for yourself.

Eve I sometimes think it's a pity that religion got any farther than "Love your neighbour as yourself": there is no other commandment greater than this. And left it at that.

Paul It's preceded if you remember, by "love God with all your heart and all your mind and all your strength".

Eve Well, I suppose in a way that *is* your neighbour. I don't know what I mean by that, but I think I think it. If those dogmatic bullies had loved this Bunyan a smitch and had a thought for his wife and family—was there a family?

Paul Yes, there was a family. His first wife had died, leaving him with four children, and the eldest of them, a girl, was blind.

Eve Was blind?

Paul He said she lay nearer to his heart than all the rest. He was tortured by the suffering he was bringing to them—felt, he said, like a man pulling the house down on the heads of his wife and children.

Eve His wife? He had married again, had he?

Paul Yes, he had married again: a girl of sixteen, called Elizabeth. The shock of his arrest sent her into premature labour and the baby died.

The Lights in the room flicker and dim

George Hullo! Is there thunder around? It's as well to be prepared, to have a stock of candles when a storm is crouching ready to spring.

The Lights steady again

Eve Perhaps something interfered with the power line. Suppose an owl had flown into it—could that be? Or the branch of a tree brushing against the wire.

Adam We take it so much for granted, the light we see by.

Paul And then something says it's not really like that; don't count on it.

The Lights flicker again

Adam It's the dark fighting to come back. It will win in the end, I expect.

The Receptionist rouses

Receptionist Eh? What's going on?

George It's more like what's going off.

Paul How's the candle power in this place, Tim?

Adam Of course: *Tim*. The time-man. We might have guessed.

Receptionist There were plenty where I was just now.

Paul You've been dreaming, old man, dreaming.

Receptionist That's as maybe. There were plenty of candles there. In the *Swan*, I think it was.

The Lights go out. There is a little light from the night sky through a window

Adam Hey-ho! That's it. The owl has landed.
Receptionist I'll call the High Sheriff. (*He lifts the phone receiver and dials*)
George The who?
Receptionist (*waving the receiver*) It's dead.
George So is he, I shouldn't wonder.
Paul It's a very strange thing, friends, Tim mentioning the *Swan*. I'll tell you why. What was I telling you before the lights got nervous?
Eve About Elizabeth, the girl Bunyan married.
Paul That's right—and a gutsy girl she was. She travelled up to London for the first time in her life, to present a petition to the Earl of Bedford, asking for John's release. The case was postponed until the next Assizes at Bedford, and there she was, bless her, making a last bid, when the Judges were sitting at the *Swan* hotel. What have you been dreaming, Tim, to make you mention the *Swan*?

Elizabeth Bunyan appears in the dark

Although a little light from the street reaches her, no-one on the stage sees her

Receptionist Well, it's you who is saying I've been dreaming. And you feel quite sure that you're awake, I suppose?
Elizabeth It's false. It's very false.
Receptionist There are things to be said for and against. The facts of the matter can be very misleading.
Paul You think so?
Receptionist Everything is so very unlikely.
Elizabeth The indictment is false. I make bold to come to you again to know what will be done with my husband. They jailed him before there was any law forbidding the meetings. He only wishes to follow his calling and live in peace.
Receptionist It's only a step, you see, between real and unreal. But how dreadfully reality gets punished for it.
Elizabeth I was with child when my husband was first apprehended—and the news of it so dismayed me I fell into labour—it lasted for eight days until the baby was born. And the baby died.
Eve What am I hearing? Is there something going on in the street?
George (*looking out*) Not a soul about. No lights in the houses.
Receptionist There were plenty of candles alight in the *Swan*, but there was so much stir in the air they danced and guttered. It was the crowding together of human breath. The candlewax ran down like tears.
Elizabeth I have four small step-children: one is blind: we have nothing to live on except what comes from my husband's work.

Eve (*to Paul*) I can't get that Elizabeth girl out of my mind! What can they have been living on while he was in prison? There couldn't have been much put by. He was a tinker, you said.

Paul Like his father before him.

Elizabeth And because he's a tinker and a poor man, he is despised and can't have justice.

Receptionist There was a great puff of scorn from the Sheriff, and the candle flames bowed so low to him they threatened to leave us in darkness.

Adam (*to Paul*) And all because he was an unlicensed preacher.

Paul Preaching according to what he called the small measure of light that God had given him. That set the Judges snapping at his heels—for doing harm to his neighbours, they said.

Elizabeth No, my Lord, it is not so. God has owned him and done much good by him.

Paul They even said his preaching was the doctrine of the Devil.

Elizabeth My Lord, when the righteous judge shall appear it will be known that his words are not the doctrine of the Devil.

Eve What a wild invention that is, making a Grimm's fairy-tale character out of the necessary dark.

George The necessary dark?

Eve Isn't that what you said? To make the creative power there must be the two: the contenders.

Paul Bunyan believed Satan was real—and gave us Apollyon.

Adam Well, as a metaphor, yes.

Paul And he got criticised at the time for dealing in metaphors. But they were metaphors for living truths. Despair was no less despair for appearing as a giant.

Elizabeth My Lord, it is another two years before the next Assize—what will become of us? And always the fearful thought in our hearts that he might be transported or put to death for knowing God as he feels he must. Always the fear of what will become of us. It's a hard thing to bear, my Lord—a hard thing to bear.

Elizabeth's voice fades and she disappears into the dark

Receptionist And then all the candle flames gave up trying, and the dark was too heavy to go on sleeping—if that's the way you see it.

Paul And then the power failed and brought you back to us.

Adam But he got the better of the giant Despair—I seem to remember—or somehow escaped from his dungeon. But for Bunyan, I suppose, it wasn't so easy.

Paul For twelve years, more or less, they kept him in jail—and at last he came to the delectable mountains of having written a best-seller—sold for eighteen pence a copy—and there, like any mountain, it has stood secure, looking out over the human scene, for the past three hundred years.

The electric power is restored, raising a cheer from all of them

There you are, Tim—you have the permission of the Electricity Board to go to sleep again.

Adam Wherever time will take you. When you're little, a week seems a terribly long time to wait for something. And even when you're much older, a century still speaks of history. But then, I imagine, time gets its skates on. An old chap once told me that when you get to eighty it's like having breakfast every half hour. At that rate even two thousand years becomes neighbourly.

George Some trees can live that long, or not far off it.

Eve That's true. A sequoia tree, I think it was. And yew trees and oak trees don't do so badly. When you were talking about the little big bang, Adam, I thought how the acorn does it. That sky-going eruption of branch and leaf.

Paul There's a wonderful passage by Mark Rutherford—his father had a shop in Bedford High Street—mid nineteenth century—Hale White his proper name—but Mark Rutherford when he took to the pen. I learnt it by heart once, the piece about the tree. I think I can still remember it. He said he was in a wood when something happened which was a transformation of himself and the world. It seemed to be no longer a tree away from him and apart from himself. The enclosing barriers of consciousness were removed and the text came into his mind, "Thou in me and I in Thee". The distinction of self and not-self, he said, was an illusion. He could feel the rising sap, and the fountain of life uprushing from the tree's roots; and the joy of the outbreak of the buds right up to the summit was his own. Whatever kept him separate from the tree he felt was nothing.

Adam Well done, well remembered.

Eve And thank you for remembering.

Adam Well, friends, I suppose we should be making our way.

George It was a good coming-together.

Eve (*to Adam*) How are your hands feeling?

Adam (*closing and opening his hands*) My own again, I think they are.

Eve So this time, perhaps you'll be able to tell me where we're heading for.

Adam That could be. I'll take a chance on it.

Holding hands, Adam and Eve begin to make their goodbyes, when George stops them

George Paul, are you hearing what I'm hearing? Listen!

The faint sound of the bells in the bell-tower ringing

Paul The bells! Who in the world could be ringing the bells? Tim, do you know anything about this? Who on earth can be ringing the bells?
Receptionist Well now, do I know? Who could be ringing the bells? The generations, it might be. It could be the generations ringing.

The others all turn towards the window to listen as the bells ring out bravely

The Curtain *falls*

FURNITURE AND PROPERTY LIST

Further dressing may be added at the director's discretion

On stage: Desk. *On it*: bell, phone
              3 chairs

LIGHTING PLOT

Property fittings required: nil
1 interior. The same throughout

To open: Night-time lighting

Cue 1   **Paul**: "…and the baby died."   (Page 9)
               Flicker and dim lights

Cue 2   **George**: "…crouching ready to spring."   (Page 9)
               Bring lights back to normal

Cue 3   **Paul**: "…don't count on it."   (Page 9)
               Flicker lights

Cue 4   **Receptionist**: "In the *Swan*, I think it was."   (Page 9)
               Black-out; bring up light of night sky through window

Cue 5   **Paul**: "…for the past three hundred years."   (Page 12)
               Bring up normal lighting

EFFECTS PLOT